So Now What?

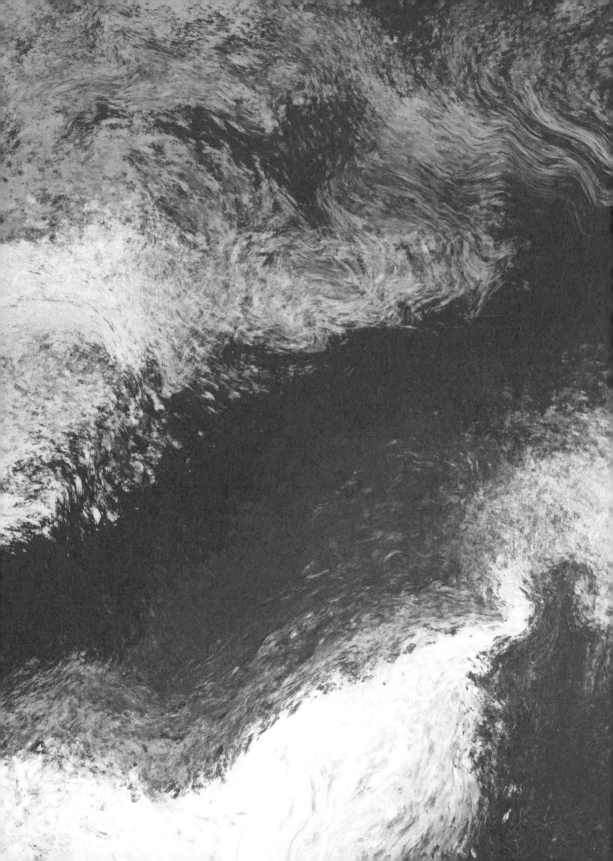

So Now What?

A GUIDED WORKBOOK TO GET UNSTUCK

CATHERINE A. BRENNAN

CONTENTS

INTRODUCTION

You want to look good, feel good, and do good. You want to be able to move through life with energy and vitality, manage your emotions with understanding and maturity, and have a sense of purpose, hope, and peace.

It's all possible.

Stuck: we all experience it. We find ourselves sad, without energy or hope. We bump up against a wall and don't know what to do next. We feel cornered as our health fails, our relationships crumble, or we don't get our head around what's in front of us. We're stuck.

Stuck is a place where we're confused, overwhelmed, or trapped. Moving seems like attempting to walk the high wire across Niagara Falls; our feet, mind, and heart fail us. There seems to be no solution, so we resign ourselves to the status quo and shrink back from the challenge.

This is stuck.

When we are stuck, we live a humdrum life. We play it safe and aren't able to fully enjoy the benefits of who we were created to be—and neither is anyone else.

Unstuck is a place of physical strength, limberness, and energy. You can function in your life without restrictions, feel well rested, live an active life, and enjoy the food you eat.

Unstuck is being mentally strong, with relationships beyond simple agreement. It's the ability to meet challenges, have a confident sense of self, think with a positive mind, and have a good work ethic. It means being curious, strong in stressful situations, resilient in difficulty, and a pleasure to be around.

Unstuck is being spiritually content, peaceful, hopeful, joyful, loving, faithful, and grateful. It's the ability to find meaning in the events of life, not being threatened by others' differing beliefs, and being part of the fabric of humanity by embracing others and self. Unstuck is concerned with others and living with a purpose.

Does this sound too good to be true?

It's not.

Buying this guided workbook is a great way to get unstuck. Taking the time to go through these questions will allow you to see clearly why you're there and what it will take to change.

The work it will take to change your stuck behaviors is easier than staying stuck. It's critically important to chew on this fact. It will be easier to lose those ten pounds and keep them off than to think about that extra weight for the rest of your life. It will be easier to forgive the person who did you wrong than to carry around the burden of hatred and revenge. And it will be easier to accept the things you don't yet understand than to try to chase down logic to neatly categorize all of life's events.

Whether you're stuck physically, mentally, or spiritually, the answer lies in becoming strong and free. Freedom exists when we are equally healthy in our body, mind, and spirit.

This combination is explosive.

This guidebook is all about you. As you delve into these questions, you will discover the reasons you are stuck. Stop trying to be "right," and instead be honest. Uncover what's been buried. Dig, dig, dig.

It might be painful. You may feel completely exposed. This is where the magic happens.

You can't change what you don't acknowledge. But when you confront the truth, you'll be able to say, "... So now what?" When you get to the root of what isn't working in your life, you can concentrate on what it will take to change.

It's all about your well-being. As you become more energetic, positive, and hopeful, your troubles will get smaller. The truths you uncover will be met with attention to your body, mind, and spirit. Physical goals must be embraced both mentally and spiritually. Mental health is enhanced with physical and spiritual strength. And the expansion of your spirit flows easily as you feel capable in your body and mind.

Writing out your answers to these questions is your way to freedom. This is your guide, and the answers will become evident as you write your observations. Something fascinating happens when you write things down: The truth is sorted out, and you go deeper into your mind. The words stare back at you, revealing their truth.

It's right there in black and white.

As you go through the questions, go beyond the obvious. You may come up with your own follow-up questions to dig deeper. Think about your physical, mental, and spiritual health. How are each of these impacting your answers?

Some of the questions in this book may not be for you. If you have healthy beliefs, you may not need to reflect on those questions. Also, it's not necessary to go in order. If you've read my book *So Now What? A Guide for People Who Feel Stuck*, you can jump to any section that you would like to dig deeper into.

I suggest going though only one set of questions a day. This is deep work, and it may overwhelm you. It's important to take away one or two lessons at a time so you can remember them clearly.

Are you ready?

Let's discover the *so now what?*

WHAT GETS US STUCK?

We get stuck because of our fears, feelings, and beliefs, as well as our desire to control and our lack of skills. We stay there because of the bad habits we develop while we're stuck. But the ultimate reason we are stuck is our unwillingness to do something about it.

Chapter One

FEAR

Fear sets up barriers to keep us from harm. That's all fine and good, except that we've allowed fear to take charge and get way out of hand. In an effort to avoid all discomfort, we also avoid opportunities, growth, and joy. We go to the same awful place in our minds when someone looks at us sideways, as if our long-time friend said they never want to see us again. The same gut-wrenching fight-or-flight sensation in our belly that should be reserved for real danger takes over our body even when no real harm exists.

Fear will get us stuck too. It can be powerful if we let it. But it's just hyperbole. Like the drama queen in high school, fear makes a big deal about all kinds of things that aren't big deals at all. She's full of hot air and just trying to get attention.

And like junk food, it's bad for us.

Fear has the power to direct our lives toward a small little corner. It's confining. Instead of offering freedom, it suspects a boogeyman around every corner. Nothing is safe, so why venture out? Fear leads us to believe there are bad consequences to every situation, so we limit our activities, attitudes, and hope. When we live in fear, our world gets small.

Fear wears us down. It changes who we are, holds us captive, and causes us to limit our experiences.

When you take a good look at where you're stuck, fear is probably at the core.

Ask yourself these questions and get honest in your heart and mind. Go to the root. This is where you'll begin to find freedom.

◇ What are you really afraid of?

_____

_____

_____

◇ Now dig deeper.

   a) Where does your fear come from?

_____

_____

_____

_____

   b) What are you specifically afraid will happen in this situation?

_____

_____

_____

_____

c) If the thing you fear happened, what would be the worst result?

_____

_____

_____

d) So now what? What is the first step you will take away from this fear?

_____

_____

_____

Try asking these four questions for another fear. And another. And another, until it becomes habit.

FEAR OF FAILURE

Fear of failure will get you stuck.

News flash—everyone fails. Even you. It may be uncomfortable, but it's a common human experience. It's not out of the ordinary or avoidable. To get better at anything, you must do it, and fail at it, over and over until you get it right.

Because failure is necessary to getting better, the first thing to get good at is failure. The first step to improving your life is to embrace your foibles, failings, and frailties.

The fear of failure causes us to try protecting ourselves from the very thing that will make our lives better. The fear of failure isn't protecting you—it's limiting you. It doesn't protect your life but only limits the possibilities. And you're stuck living in a place filled with excuses and fear.

Freedom comes when you're willing to fail until you succeed.

◇   How do you define failure in yourself?

_____

_____

_____

_____

_____

◇   What are you afraid to fail at?

_____

_____

_____

_____

◇   What could failing teach you?

_____

_____

_____

_____

◇ What are you gaining by holding onto a fear of failure?

_____

_____

_____

_____

_____

◇ What are you losing by holding onto a fear of failure?

_____

_____

_____

_____

_____

◇ What good things are the fear of failure keeping you from?

_____

_____

_____

_____

_____

Although none of us want to be wrong, all of us sometimes are. It's part of being human.

But when the normal mistakes of life become so frightening that they stop us from being ourselves, we're prone to getting stuck. The fear of being wrong takes precedence, and we walk on eggshells to avoid looking silly. Being unable to accept our weakness makes us weak.

The fear of being wrong begs the question, why do we expect to always be right? It's a good one to ponder. We must go after the source of our discomfort to avoid the fear. Thinking through this will certainly cause the impossible standard to dissipate. Then we will walk in the freedom we all desire.

◊　What are you afraid of being wrong about?

_____

_____

_____

_____

◊　What specifically are you afraid would happen if you were wrong?

_____

_____

_____

_____

◇ Why do you expect to always be right?

_____

_____

_____

_____

_____

◇ What reactions do you have when you're wrong?

_____

_____

_____

_____

_____

◇ What is your fear of being wrong keeping you from?

_____

_____

_____

_____

_____

Most of us care to some degree about what others think of us. It's normal to want positive feedback. The question is, how much power does it have?

If we aren't careful, trying to please others at our own expense becomes a habit.

We can care too much about what others think of us when we don't feel good about ourselves. Are you allowing strangers to determine your worth?

When we're driven by other people's thoughts instead of our own, the fear of being wrong in another's eyes, regardless of who they are, has us chasing an elusive legitimacy.

And we're stuck.

◇   How is the concern about what others think about you directing your actions?

_____

_____

_____

_____

_____

◇   Whose opinions do you value over your own? Why?

_____

_____

_____

_____

_____

◇ Why is it easier to listen to someone else rather than yourself?

_____

_____

_____

_____

_____

FEAR OF AUTHENTICITY

The fear of being authentic leads to us being . . . inauthentic.

The world needs _you_. It needs the authentic, unedited, raw version of you.

We pretend all kinds of things in order to be accepted. When we pretend to be someone else, we leave people in our lives unsure about who we really are. This leads to all kinds of confusion. We get stuck when we do what we think others want us to do instead of doing what comes naturally to us.

Freedom is being who we truly are.

◇ What characteristics are you faking that aren't really you?

_____

_____

_____

◇ Who are you pretending to be? Why?

_____

_____

_____

_____

_____

◇   What would it take to stop pretending to be someone you're not?

_____

_____

_____

◇   What would it take for you to know you're "enough" and be free?

_____

_____

_____

_____

FEAR OF MAKING THINGS WORSE

When we're afraid of making things worse, ironically, we make things worse. Staying static is no solution. We must act.

If we don't try something new, we're guaranteed to keep things as they are. We won't know whether things will get better or worse until we take a step toward change. When the fear of making things worse takes over, we're bound to stay stuck.

But the fear of making things worse is unwarranted and untested. It keeps us from solutions, lessons, and success.

◇ Name something you are afraid to do because you may make things worse. What are you afraid will happen by taking this step?

_____

_____

_____

_____

◇ How could things actually get better? Come up with three ways.

_____

_____

_____

FEAR OF THE UNKNOWN

No one knows what the future has in store. We hold tight to things the way they are out of fear that change will bring about circumstances we don't know how to deal with. We can stay stuck because we cannot predict the future.

But when we learn to embrace the positive aspects of changes around us, we're more likely to adapt to the uncertain but inevitable changes which come our way.

◇ What unknown event are you afraid of? How does it have you stuck?

_____

_____

_____

_____

◇ What scares you about the unknown?

_____

_____

_____

_____

◇ How can you manage these fears of the unknown?

_____

_____

_____

◇ What opportunities are these fears of the unknown keeping you from?

_____

_____

_____

Chapter Two

FEELINGS

Our emotions are powerful. They affect not only our thoughts but also our bodies. They can cause us to slip into the mud puddle before we even know it.

What is it with those dang emotions?

When I was depressed, I bemoaned emotions altogether. They seemed to cause me nothing but trouble. But eventually, I discovered that my feelings were a signal of something inside me needing adjustment. My anger could reveal insecurity or hurt. My sadness revealed weaknesses, wrong mindsets, and disappointments.

Some very wise teaching revealed my feelings were my responsibility to take care of. All my life, I had believed others could "make" me feel a certain way, and it was their fault when I felt bad. This had me stuck.

If you have trouble managing your emotions, know that this understanding will bring you freedom. Much of the battle comes from identifying *what* feelings have you stuck.

BLAMING OTHERS

When we blame other people for our troubles, we get stuck letting them decide when we'll solve those problems.

I could write a whole book on how I have blamed other people for my problems. In an effort to avoid painful feelings, I threw blame onto someone else.

But the pain didn't go away with blame, so I stayed stuck.

The blame game is easy because there are so many people to blame for our problems. Blame is easy but unproductive. Although it may feel good in the moment, this blame gets us nowhere but stuck.

◇ Who or what are you blaming for your most difficult problem?

_____

◇ Name a problem you have in your life you consider someone else's fault. What is your part of the problem? What is one thing you can do about it now?

_____

_____

_____

_____

◇ Name something you are blaming on someone from your childhood. What have you done to take responsibility for the problem?

_____

_____

_____

_____

YOUR FEELINGS BECOME MY FEELINGS

The motivational speaker Jim Rohn famously said we are the average of the five people we spend the most time with. Who we spend time with and how we relate to them affects our life in a big way. When we hang out with people who are sick, sad, or skeptical, our feelings will become gloomy too. Unless we are strong physically, mentally, and spiritually, we will adopt the feelings of those around us.

Because of this principle, we can be unaware of how sick we are because those around us are also sick. Our friends become an unofficial measure of what it means to feel good. However, often our friends have the same weaknesses we do. The same stuck-ness. We find comfort in someone else understanding our failings. But we can stay stuck if those around us want us to stay there.

When someone in the clan chooses to be healthy, the others may seek to bring them back into the group's standard of healthy because they feel uncomfortable with change.

But a healthy person can celebrate other's differences and run their life according to their individual ideas and feelings, and not those of others.

◊ What's one behavior you have adopted because it's what your friends want you to do?

_____

◊ What are some habits and behaviors people exhibit that you would like to develop more?

_____

_____

_____

◇ What are some habits and behaviors people exhibit that you don't want to imitate?

_____

_____

_____

◇ Name at least one way you could pick up on the good habits of others and stay away from the bad ones.

_____

_____

_____

RELYING ON OUR FEELINGS TO TELL US THE TRUTH

Feelings can be fickle and aren't typically a good anchor to hook our boat to. They ebb and flow based on the weather, how much sleep we've gotten, and our expectations. We need our mind and our wisdom to drive us instead. When we rely on our feelings for direction and truth, we're following the wrong leader. Like a kite that has lost its string, we float on the winds of emotion with no determined destination. One emotion leads to another, and soon we're lost.

Our feelings, however, are a powerful signal. Like a road sign, they point out *something*. What it is, however, will take more than our feelings to discern. When we recognize what it is, we will be free.

Our feelings come not only from our thoughts but from our body. When we run low on food, we can get hangry. My body is like a toddler who screams out and makes demands whenever she's uncomfortable.

We can also "feel" bad emotionally because our spiritual muscle is weak. When hope, gratitude, joy, and love aren't at the front of our thoughts, we're prone to allow feelings of fear, thoughtlessness, unhappiness, and hatred to rule the roost.

When we realize our feelings come from all these places, we are equipped to use them for our benefit.

◇ What strong negative feelings do you have often? Where do these negative feelings come from?

_____

_____

_____

_____

_____

◇ What do you think those negative feelings are telling you?

_____

_____

_____

_____

_____

I FEEL POWERLESS TO CHANGE

Many of us feel powerless over our lives. We believe life is just how it is, and we're stuck living it in a certain way. With this internal struggle, the possibility of change seems impossible. We feel there's nothing we can do to change our circumstances or the feelings that go along with them.

I understand.

The idea that we cannot change the circumstances of our life leaves us in a weak position. This feeling of powerlessness gets us stuck. Each one of us owns our life and has the potential to make a change. The choices may seem difficult, but they are easier than living without them.

◊ What makes you feel powerless in your life?

_____

_____

_____

_____

◊ How can you overcome the feeling of powerlessness?

_____

_____

_____

_____

◇ What steps are necessary to become powerful over a difficulty that has you stuck?

_____

_____

_____

_____

_____

◇ What step will you take today?

_____

_____

_____

Chapter Three

BELIEFS

What do you believe about yourself? Are there conclusions you've drawn based on your age, gender, economic status, body build, heredity, or opportunities? Do you limit your dreams based on where you live, how much money you don't have, who you know, your grades in school, or past mistakes?

Our limiting beliefs get us stuck. To protect ourselves, we set up walls. Those walls are limiting beliefs that keep us safe from risk. They keep us from believing we can get better. They keep us locked out of trying something new and expanding who we are.

We learned many limiting beliefs as children as we listened carefully to what adults said. As we grow into adulthood, our beliefs need to grow too. We must question what we've been told and reframe our thinking to our truth. We get stuck when we fail to go through that process.

When we challenge our limiting beliefs, we take a step towards freedom.

◇ What are your limiting beliefs?

_____

_____

_____

◇ What limiting beliefs do you still carry from your childhood?

_____

_____

_____

_____

_____

◇ What opportunities have these limiting beliefs kept you from?

_____

_____

_____

_____

_____

GENDERED BELIEFS

Some limiting beliefs say there are tasks meant for men and tasks meant for women. These limit the potential of people everywhere to do what they love and offer it to the rest of us.

Men stay stuck when they back away from doing things because their limiting beliefs cause them to be afraid of looking feminine. Women's limiting beliefs can see every fix-it job around the house as her mate's responsibility. He wasn't born with a hammer in his hand, and he's not less of a man because of it.

Limiting beliefs keep us stuck.

◇ What limiting beliefs do you have because of your gender?

_____

_____

_____

_____

_____

◇ What tasks do you reserve specifically for men or for women?
What is the basis for your conclusion?

_____

_____

_____

_____

◇ What is one thing you have wanted to do but didn't because of your gender?

_____

_____

_____

_____

◇ Name a role model in your gender for the task you want to accomplish.

_____

_____

_____

_____

_____

BELIEVING IT'S A PERMANENT CONDITION

When we're stuck, it's hard to see the current situation as temporary. This is especially true when our pain is deep. We're sad, mad, or overwhelmed and have convinced ourselves we'll always feel this way.

We often let our mind wander to past hurts. This causes us to make up a story about what will happen in the future based on what happened in the past. It's a protective measure, to ensure that we are ready for the worst possible series of events and to avoid disappointment.

But our present dire circumstances may just be telling us we're stuck. Stuck with conclusions. Stuck with fear. Stuck in so many ways.

Being stuck is never a permanent condition, unless we choose to make it so.

◇ What would you describe as a permanent problem?

_____

_____

_____

_____

◇ What thoughts are you "stuck" with that have you believing in the permanency of this situation?

_____

_____

_____

_____

_____

◇ Identify one or more ways to reframe this situation from permanent to one that can be overcome.

_____

_____

_____

_____

_____

BELIEVING WE'RE NOT ENOUGH

We sometimes believe we're not enough. We look around and see what other people are accomplishing and wish we were achieving something great too. Inevitably, there is always someone more accomplished, more beautiful, and happier than we are. We will always lose when we play the comparison game.

Being "not enough" shows up in many ways. Some people berate themselves. Others say yes when they mean no. Healthy people don't think that way.

◇ How do you define being "enough" for youself?

_____

_____

_____

_____

◇ In what ways do you feel you are not enough?

_____

_____

_____

_____

◇ What thoughts and behaviors do you have that show you believe you are not enough?

_____

_____

_____

_____

◊ What is the worst thing that could happen if you started believing you are enough?

_____

_____

_____

BELIEVING THE STORIES WE MAKE UP

Making up stories and believing them as truth is another way our beliefs limit our lives and get us stuck. When we make up a story to fill in an uncomfortable gap, we convince ourselves the story is true and then seek to defend it. Our drive to have an answer trumps the truth.

When we make up a story, we are often the main character. Other people's choices and preferences get squeezed into a play where we're the star. Instead of considering that each person is inside their own play, we take their words and actions when different from our own and come up with an explanation by making up a story.

We get stuck in a whirlwind of confusion when we believe the stories we've made up.

◊ What story that may not be true have you made up in your mind about a situation?

_____

_____

_____

_____

◇ What are some other possible explanations of the situation that you may not know about?

_____

_____

_____

_____

_____

_____

◇ How will you know if the story you have created in your mind to understand a situation is true?

_____

_____

_____

_____

_____

_____

BELIEVING THE JUDGMENTS OF OTHERS

We all make mistakes, and some are bigger than others. Those mistakes can last a lifetime in our minds, which keeps us stuck. The belief that what we've done is unforgivable and will be judged by others can cause us to be stuck.

◇ What past judgment that you're holding against yourself is keeping you stuck?

_____

_____

_____

◇ What evidence do you see that the judgment you hold against yourself is not held by others any longer?

_____

_____

_____

_____

◇ Who would you be if you dropped others' judgments of your past mistakes?

_____

_____

_____

Chapter Four

CONTROL

Our attempts to force things that are out of our control leave us frustrated. We try to control the future, the present, and even the past. Our attempts to control come from a weak position and get us stuck.

WE HOLD ON TO RESENTMENT

Resentment is a nasty little emotion. Like a poisonous snake that hides in the bushes, you might not even know it's there until it reaches out to snatch your joy away. If you feed your resentment, it'll become even bigger and even more vile. Resentment doesn't allow us to regain strength and confidence. It is, however, holding you stuck in a slurry of negative emotions.

◇ What resentment are you holding that is showing you you're stuck?

_____

_____

_____

_____

◇ Why does it seem difficult to let this resentment go?

_____

_____

_____

◇ What negative emotion is your resentment feeding?

_____

_____

_____

WE HOLD ON TO REGRETS

When we continue to regret our past mistakes, we don't allow ourselves to move forward. We are stuck with the fantasy that we should have known better. We should have behaved better. We should have been better. But we're human. We didn't know better. We didn't behave better. We weren't better than we wish we had been.

Holding onto regrets is a way to continually punish yourself and keeps you stuck.

◇ What regret do you have that has you stuck?

_____

_____

_____

◇ Describe the situation you were in when you did something you regret. What do you know now that you didn't then?

_____

_____

_____

◇ What can you do today to get rid of your regret for past mistakes?

_____

_____

_____

PERFECTIONISM

Nothing's perfect. There is no perfect spouse, perfect job, perfect haircut, perfect phone, or perfect child. We know this, but we don't like to accept it. Perfectionism will always trip us up. Our attempts don't lead us closer to perfection; they crash and burn trying to meet a standard that cannot be met.

◇ What are you expecting to be perfect?

_____

_____

_____

_____

◇ How is trying to be perfect keeping you stuck?

_____

_____

_____

_____

_____

◇ What new expectations, short of perfection, will you embrace to be free?

_____

_____

_____

_____

COMPARISONS

Almost everyone plays the comparison game. We look at someone and decide they're happier, richer, wiser, or have their whole life more together than us.

But it's always a losing proposition to play this game, because there is always someone seemingly more accomplished, beautiful, or happy. Playing the comparison game gets us stuck. It causes us to focus on our insecurities and weaknesses.

◇ Who do you compare yourself to?

_____

_____

_____

_____

◇ What is a way the comparison game is keeping you stuck?

_____

_____

_____

_____

◇ What judgments do you carry against yourself because of the
comparison game?

_____

_____

_____

_____

◇ What attributes or feelings go along with those negative judgments of yourself?

_____

_____

_____

_____

STUBBORNNESS

Another way we try to control the present is stubbornness—showing dogged determination not to change our attitude or position on something, especially in spite of good arguments or reasons to do so.

When we're stubborn, we're rigid, like a board. Strength is good, but inflexibility ensures no movement will take place. When push comes to shove, a stiff board will snap in two.

It takes humility to let go of stubbornness. Accepting new information will get us unstuck.

◇ What stubborn ideas are keeping you stuck in unhealthy ways of living?

_____

_____

_____

_____

◇ What is another explanation for your stubborn thought? Be creative!

_____

_____

_____

_____

_____

◇ What can help you be aware you are being stubborn?

_____

_____

_____

_____

_____

UNREALISTIC EXPECTATIONS

We can get frustrated when the circumstances, the economy, or our partners don't live up to our expectations. Our frustration, however, is just a sign that our expectations aren't matching reality and we are waiting for them to line up—but, in truth, we are stuck.

It's okay to come up with our own expectations for spirituality, cleanliness, friendships, health, and life, but it is unrealistic to require others to follow suit. It's only when we allow others to be different that we can be free of unrealistic expectations.

◇ What unrealistic expectations do you have for yourself or others?

_____

_____

_____

_____

◇ How do those unrealistic expectations get you stuck?

_____

_____

_____

_____

◇ What is a way to make your unrealistic expectations be more realistic?

_____

_____

_____

_____

Chapter Five

SKILLS

WE DON'T KNOW WHAT TO DO

Another reason we stay stuck is that, even though we know we're stuck, we just don't know what to do next.

Figuring out what to do requires a lot of trial and error. Not everything we try is helpful to get us unstuck. We must be open to all the possibilities. Remember, you do not need to stay stuck. There is always a solution, and you are the one who will benefit the most by finding it.

◇ Describe a problem that you do not have a current solution to. If time or money were no object, how could you solve this problem?

_____

_____

_____

_____

_____

◇ What are some resources you could seek out to solve a problem you don't know how to deal with?

_____

_____

_____

◇ What are some things you have tried to solve your problem? Do you know why they didn't work?

_____

_____

_____

_____

◇ Do you believe you can find the answer to your problems? If not, who can help you find the answer?

_____

_____

_____

_____

WE DON'T HAVE THE SKILLS TO GET UNSTUCK

Having an open mind and the humility to change is imperative to getting unstuck. There is always a way to improve our circumstances, and that way may include learning a new skill. There is no age at which we've learned all we can.

These skills don't necessarily come along naturally. Just because you're eighteen years old and classified as an adult does not mean you know how to take care of your body. Just because you are married and have children doesn't mean you have the mental health skills to be a good parent. And just because you're retired and have had a successful career does not mean you have a well-rounded understanding of life.

How do you get the skills to get unstuck? You're going to have to learn them! Without the effort to learn a new skill, you will stay stuck. These skills may be difficult at first, but learning them will be easier than staying stuck.

◇ What new skills will you try to get unstuck?

_____

_____

_____

_____

_____

◇ How will you learn these new skills? How long will it take to master them?

_____

_____

_____

◇ What beliefs must change in your mind to learn the new skills needed to get you unstuck?

_____

_____

_____

WE'RE FOCUSED ON WHAT WE DON'T HAVE

When we focus simply on what we don't have, we won't see a complete picture. Our vision is limited. When we see the glass as half empty, we focus on what we don't have instead of what we do. If your focus is on scarcity, it's a sure sign you're stuck.

This is just a bad habit.

◇ What are you focusing on that you don't have?

_____

_____

_____

_____

◇ Turn what you don't have around. What _do_ you have?

_____

_____

_____

◇ How will you change your focus from what you don't have to what you do have?

_____

_____

_____

_____

WE TAKE THE BAIT

We may be stuck because we're taking the bait from a sick, sad, or skeptical person. They are stuck and want us to join them in their mud puddle. They sit with their fishing rod and throw bait out in front of us. It can be juicy gossip or anger toward a common enemy. This bait can draw us in like a fish to a minnow and cause us to get stuck.

◇ What bait have you taken which has you stuck?

_____

_____

_____

◇ Why is the bait people throw out to you in your mud puddle so juicy?

_____

_____

_____

◇ How will you recognize the good-for-nothing bait the next time it's tempting you?

_____

_____

_____

_____

_____

Chapter Six

BAD THINGS WE DO WHILE WE'RE STUCK

We can get into some bad habits while we're stuck. This is normal because we mindlessly repeat behaviors because of their familiarity. Recognizing these bad habits will help us identify that we're stuck. They are a sign we need to make a plan to get unstuck. Addressing our bad habits is the way forward.

WE COMPLAIN

Complaining gives a voice to our unhappiness. This feeds negative intentions and emotion. As tangible as a hammer hitting a nail, those words have power. They fan the flames of discontent in our heart. Those complaints are a sure sign we are stuck.

◇ What is one thing you complain about?

_____

_____

_____

◇ What does your complaining serve?

_____

_____

_____

_____

_____

◇ What is the opposite of complaining?

_____

_____

_____

_____

_____

◇ What would not complaining serve?

_____

_____

_____

_____

_____

WE HYPERBOLIZE

Sometimes we exaggerate our plight as a coping mechanism. It's both tolerated and accepted in our culture. But hyperbole isn't a skill you want to develop, and using it won't help you get unstuck. Listening to it won't either. Exaggeration simply exacerbates the problem. This negative energy gets you stuck.

◇ What words are you using to exaggerate a situation?

_____

_____

_____

◇ What are you trying to accomplish by exaggerating a situation?

_____

_____

_____

◇ Does exaggerating a situation help you to cope with your problem? Explain why or why not.

_____

_____

_____

_____

_____

WE GET PESSIMISTIC

Because of our twenty-four-hour appetite for breaking news, we often find out about horrible events. There is no doubt these tragedies are awful and take a cruel toll on humankind. The details of these rare events are noxious, and feeding the curious but twisted part of us will lead us straight to a dead end. The amount of sad news we take in each day can lead us into thinking our lives are filled with potential perils. The bizarre becomes commonplace and our pessimism grows.

The excess coverage and details are causing personal damage and making us stuck. We're becoming fearful, anxiety worn, and cynical about each event's outcome.

It can also lead us to make poor choices as we feed on the bad news du jour. These poor choices leave us stuck, and we're not free.

◇ What are you pessimistic about?

_____

_____

_____

◇ Where did your pessimism come from?

_____

_____

_____

_____

◇ How is pessimism keeping you stuck? Would you like to be less pessimistic? How can that happen?

_____

_____

_____

_____

_____

WE IGNORE OUR PROBLEMS

Ignoring our problems doesn't make them go away; it starts a snowball effect. One problem sticks to another, creating an even bigger problem. Suddenly, the problem becomes so big it seems impossible to face.

By ignoring the problem, things become worse, not better.

◇ What small problems are you not addressing that could create a snowball effect?

_____

_____

_____

◇ When you put off problems in your life, what effect does it have?

_____

_____

_____

_____

_____

◇ Name one goal, task, or obligation you have put off and describe the results.

_____

_____

_____

_____

_____

Chapter Seven

MORE REASONS WE'RE STUCK

There are a few more reasons we're stuck, and they have to do with unhealthy mindsets. The good news is that once we realize our wrong thinking, we can shift to a more productive attitude. Facing these unprofitable ways of thinking is a surefire way to get unstuck.

WE WON'T TAKE A STEP

We are stuck simply because we won't take a step. We may be waiting for someone else to fix our problems. Or we lack the courage, energy, or self-love it will take.

◇   What small step could you take to get unstuck?

_____

_____

_____

_____

◇ Why haven't you taken a step to get unstuck?

_____

_____

_____

_____

_____

_____

◇ What explanations, beliefs, or excuses are you using that keep you from taking a step to get unstuck?

_____

_____

_____

_____

_____

_____

WE'RE WAITING FOR SOMEONE ELSE TO RESCUE US

Just like Sleeping Beauty, who slept until Prince Charming awakened her, many of us live like we are damsels in distress. We wait for someone else to take us out of our misery and improve our lives.

Except it's *our* life.

◇ Who are you expecting to swoop in and pull you out of your problems? How long have you been waiting for them to help?

_____

_____

_____

_____

_____

◇ What control do you have over your problem that no one else has?

_____

_____

_____

_____

_____

WE DON'T HAVE THE COURAGE TO STEP FORWARD

The definition of courage is *the ability to do something that frightens one*, or *strength in the face of pain or grief*.

When we don't have the courage to do something that needs to be done, we are stuck.

Our lack of courage to face the pain and grief keeps us stuck. You must believe me when I tell you this principle. There is freedom on the other side of it. The battle may seem difficult, but being stuck in it is more difficult yet.

To get unstuck, you have to muster up enough courage to face your pain and grief.

◇ What is it you haven't had the courage to do?

_____

_____

_____

_____

◇ What is the worst possible thing that could happen if you took a courageous step?

_____

_____

_____

_____

◇ What would you gain by taking a courageous step?

_____

_____

_____

_____

WE WON'T ENGAGE IN SELF-CARE

Self-care does not mean you have manicures weekly, sleep fourteen hours a day, and only do what you want to do. Self-care is living your life in the healthiest way possible. It means you consider what you eat as fuel for your life. It means you protect yourself from people who drain you emotionally. It means you invest time in prayer or meditation.

A lack of self-care is probably the biggest reason many of us stay stuck.

◇ What self-care are you lacking?

_____

_____

_____

◇ Why is it difficult to engage in self-care?

_____

_____

_____

_____

◇ What would you gain if you engaged in self-care?

_____

_____

_____

◇ What would those around you gain if you engaged in self-care?

_____

_____

_____

WE WON'T GROW UP

Our parents did the best they could. Unfortunately, many of us didn't get what we needed as children because our parents didn't have the skills to give it. This can cause a lifetime of pain. We got stuck because we weren't loved, nurtured, or cared for properly. We grow into adults and carry the pain with us.

It's reasonable to feel the pain when you're a child, but as you become an adult, these emotional pains become your responsibility. The pain can be a sticking point if it isn't dealt with. Seeing your parents as flawed human beings, just like you are, is a big step toward getting unstuck.

To get unstuck, we need to start acting like an adult.

◇ How are you still acting like a child in your relationship with your parents?

_____

_____

_____

◇ What can you do if your parents still want you to be the child?

_____

_____

_____

◇ How can you become more independent and have a healthy adult/adult relationship with your parents?

_____

_____

_____

_____

_____

◇ How are you still acting like a parent in your relationship with your adult sons and daughters?

_____

_____

_____

_____

◇ What can you do if your children still want you to be the parent?

_____

_____

_____

_____

◇ How can you become more independent and have a healthy adult/adult relationship with your adult sons and daughters?

_____

_____

_____

_____

_____

WE WON'T GO TO THE EFFORT OF CHANGING THINGS

Children can find it hard to clean their room because it's too big. It seems like it will take a year to put all their toys away. Even though the consequences may mean no TV time, they won't clean because it looks like it will take too much effort.

As adults, we can be stuck too because it seems too darn hard to make things better. Even if we believe things can improve, the effort may seem too daunting. We won't make an effort.

When we won't take a step to change, we're stuck.

◇ What have you not been willing to do that has you stuck?

_____

_____

_____

_____

_____

◇ Describe the effort it will take to get unstuck. Break it down into small steps.

_____

_____

_____

_____

_____

◇ If you took the steps to get unstuck, how could your life be different?

_____

_____

_____

_____

_____

WHY GET UNSTUCK?

We know we're stuck but the thought of change is daunting.
We understand things aren't working for us but at least they're familiar.
We want to look better. We want to feel better. We want to do better.

What is being stuck in an unhealthy body keeping you from? Energy to do the things you want? Good sleep? Clothes you feel good in? A positive self-image? A positive attitude? Flexibility? Strength? A strong immune system? Clear thinking?

What is being stuck with emotional baggage keeping you from? Happiness? Opportunity? Healthy relationships? Confidence? Solutions? Laughter? Freedom? Ownership?

What is skepticism keeping you from? Love? Joy? Hope? Understanding? Peace? Certainty? Gratefulness? Meaning?

At what cost?

◇ What is stuck keeping you from?

_____

_____

_____

_____

_____

◇ How would your life look if you were not stuck from these things?

_____

_____

_____

_____

_____

_____

◇ How will you recognize you are stuck?

_____

_____

_____

_____

_____

_____

Chapter Eight

WHAT WILL IT TAKE?

IT'S A WORTHY EFFORT

Getting unstuck takes time. It takes change. Our old ways will need to be discarded for good. It has to be done.

Being stuck takes effort too. It's difficult, burdensome, and tiring. It has you exhausted, frustrated, and blue. Make no mistake, it's hard work to stay in the mud puddle, splashing around in the dysfunction that put you there. Wouldn't you like to get out?

To gain freedom, a revolution has to happen. It doesn't have to be dramatic and treacherous. Just change. Something new. Small steps. One little adjustment in how you go about your day. Followed by another. The steps will be tough. But it's tougher not to take them.

◇   What hard work are you enduring by staying stuck?

_____

_____

_____

◊ What step will you take today to get unstuck? What kind of effort will it take?

_____

_____

_____

_____

_____

◊ How will you stay motivated to continue the effort to get unstuck?

_____

_____

_____

_____

_____

BELIEVE YOU CAN CHANGE

To get unstuck, you must believe you can get there. If you don't believe you can change who you are in a relationship, open your heart to faith, lose those extra ten pounds, or reach a goal, you won't.

It's absolutely necessary for you to believe it.

It can be hard to try something new when all else has failed. The belief that it can be done, however, is your only way to freedom.

◇ Do you believe you can change? Why or why not?

_____

_____

_____

_____

◇ What reasons or explanations do you have for being stuck?

_____

_____

_____

_____

◇ What beliefs match your reasons for being stuck?

_____

_____

_____

_____

SUCCESS

People do not become successful without paying a price. Their success is a by-product of a bunch of healthy habits, one on top of the other, that elevate them to success.

◇ What habits could lead you to success?

_____

_____

_____

_____

◇ What keeps you from embracing the habits that lead to success?

_____

_____

_____

_____

◇ What is a creative way to remind yourself of one successful habit for thirty days?

_____

_____

_____

_____

TAKE ACTION

It would be nice if our problems just disappeared overnight. But they don't. It takes action to get unstuck.

Swallow that reality.

Change is necessary and it's up to you. It's important to keep in mind that it's easier to develop a good habit than live with a bad one.

◇ What teeny-tiny little action could you take to get unstuck?

_____

_____

_____

◇ What ways would the action to get unstuck show love to yourself?

_____

_____

_____

_____

_____

◇ Explain why taking a step to get unstuck is a worthy effort.

_____

_____

_____

Chapter Nine

CHANGE IS EASIER WITH THE HELP OF OTHERS

ENCOURAGEMENT

Something tangible happens when a person shows us encouragement. Our heart flutters, we feel their support, and we know we're not alone. Everything is easier when we receive encouragement.

Encouraging words can give us the confidence to take a step away from being stuck. They can be just enough fuel to help us. Like a cold glass of water on a hot summer day, they will refresh us and give us what it takes to move forward.

◇ Who in your life gives you encouraging words?

_____

_____

_____

_____

◇ What encouraging words would you like to hear?

_____

_____

_____

_____

_____

◇ How can you get more encouraging people in your life?

_____

_____

_____

_____

WISDOM

Transformation from our place of stuck can be easier with a well-placed piece of wisdom. It can come from the simplest of places. We need to keep our ears and hearts open to the wisdom all around us.

◇ Where is an unexpected place to find wisdom?

_____

_____

_____

◇ List the people who have given you wise words. Recall what they said.

_____

_____

_____

_____

_____

◇ List a wise saying that inspires you. Why is it wise? What does it mean to you?

_____

_____

_____

_____

_____

COACH

We can be challenged by a coach now and then to get unstuck. It can be something as simple as a math problem we can't figure out or as complex as whether to continue a relationship.

◇ How have people coached you in the past? What was the result?

_____

_____

_____

_____

_____

◇ What topic would you like to be coached on?

_____

_____

_____

_____

◇ Who could you ask to coach you today?

_____

_____

_____

_____

HOW TO GET UNSTUCK

You've got the power, but how do you access it? What steps do you take? Where do you start? Although this can seem overwhelming, it does not need to be. You're stuck now, and you are making it day to day. All you need to do is take a step away from an unhealthy habit that is making your life difficult.

To make a change, you're going to have to take a step. Any step will do. Some will be easier for you and some will be hard. It's always that way.

Everyone has a body, mind, and spirit. All three areas must be in good working order to get unstuck. How will you access your power? By improving how your body, mind, and spirit operate. What steps will you take? The ones you need to. Your plan will be different from anyone else's.

The motivation is up to you. It's your body, your mind, your spirit, and your life.

How do you get unstuck? Be committed to yourself. Love yourself more than anyone else does. Take a step forward to be free.

Chapter Ten

FREE YOUR BODY

One of the things that makes humans unique is our ability to use tools. We drive cars to get from point A to point B; we use computers to communicate and calculate; we use hammers and levels to build a wall.

Take a look at yourself in the mirror. Imagine you could grab your hips, pull your whole body over your head, and set it next to you. Take a look at it. It's just your body. Think of it as a tool. It needs to be fed, moved, and given rest to perform well. Your body deserves love and needs your care. It's the only body you have. You live in it every single day.

FEED YOUR BODY

You are what you eat. It was a popular saying in the seventies, and it's still true.

But what are we supposed to eat? Is fat good or bad for us? Carbs or no carbs? Do we need to take supplements? Many people throw up their hands in frustration. I get it. Let's talk about the parts of this that will help you to navigate these tricky waters.

First of all, it's our responsibility to eat right. It's not the surgeon general's, Dr. Oz's, or our spouse's. If we get sick because our immune system is weak, the surgeon general isn't going to suffer, we are.

When we eat right, food fuels our body in amazing ways. How do you choose what to eat?

◇ How would you like to choose what you eat?

_____

_____

_____

◇ On a scale of 1–10, how responsible are you being with your food choices? Why?

_____

_____

_____

_____

◇ What would have to change for you to eat what is good for your body most of the time?

_____

_____

_____

_____

Each of our bodies has basically the same functions, but they are infinitely complex. Some people can eat lots of food and not gain weight, while others struggle if they look at a piece of chocolate cake out of the corner of their eye. Some like the heat and others prefer cold. Some wake up energetic in the morning and others gain steam at the end of the day. Our bodies function differently, and we need to let the comparisons go, stop the jealousy, and focus on our own diet.

◊ What foods make you feel good? (physically/mentally/spiritually)

_____

_____

_____

_____

_____

◊ What foods make you feel bad? (physically/mentally/spiritually)

_____

_____

_____

_____

_____

◇ Would you describe eating food as a spiritual experience? Explain.

_____

_____

_____

_____

_____

◇ What foods do you crave? Are these foods good for you?

_____

_____

_____

_____

_____

Each year, scientists discover more about how food affects our bodies. We are not done learning yet! As our bodies age, they require more or less of different foods. Our planet has changed too. We have new foods available that may or may not be good for us. And government policy sets the direction of prices and availability of foods. We need to stay in the game and figure out what works for *our* body.

◇ How have your eating habits changed over time?

_____

_____

_____

_____

◇ What are you eating now that you weren't eating ten years ago that is having a positive impact on your body, mind, and spirit?

_____

_____

_____

_____

◇ What are you eating now that you weren't eating ten years ago that is having a negative impact on your body, mind, and spirit?

_____

_____

_____

_____

_____

Foods have all kinds of effects on our mood. Even the most positive person can be in distress because of their lack of calories. Everything we put in our mouth will affect how our body feels and, therefore, affect our emotions. Pay attention.

◇ What emotional changes can you tie to eating a certain food?

_____

_____

_____

_____

◇ How long are your emotions satisfied by eating comfort foods?
Is it worth it?

_____

_____

_____

_____

◇ What emotions would you like to feed with your eating habits?

_____

_____

_____

_____

◇ What foods give you extra energy?

_____

_____

_____

_____

MOVE YOUR BODY

We were created to move. Watch a toddler all day and you'll see how natural it is for them to stay in motion. Watch an ant, a squirrel, or a dog. They don't stop unless they are eating or sleeping.

We need to move too. As a society we are realizing the pendulum has shifted too far to the side of sedentary, and we need to move into a more active routine.

On top of all the technology that reduces our movement, many of us sit at desks and work long hours, finding no time to stroll in the park. We jump in our cars and go from here to there, stopping at a drive-through to pick up dinner and then race home and collapse on the couch. The thought of walking a mile or two each day seems crazy and doesn't fit our lifestyle.

What are we to do? Take one small step at a time.

◇ What stops you from moving enough?

_____

_____

_____

_____

◇ What small step could you take to move your body more?

_____

_____

_____

_____

_____

◇ What do you believe are the costs and/or benefits of movement/exercise?

_____

_____

_____

_____

_____

◇ How do you think you would feel if you moved more?

_____

_____

_____

_____

REST YOUR BODY

Let's talk about sleep. We all need it. Without it, we can't function properly. It's a precious commodity, and so many things assault this area of our lives. To get unstuck, we must get serious about our sleep and protect it like a precious diamond.

How much sleep is enough? Most people need between seven and nine hours per night. Interestingly, professional athletes, musicians, chess players, and actors get on average eight hours and thirty-six minutes of sleep a night. That's an hour and a half more than the average American.

Maybe that's why they're professionals.

◇ How much sleep would it take for you to feel rested each morning?

_____

◇ When you do not get enough sleep, how does it affect your day?

_____

_____

_____

_____

It's important not to allow children to dictate sleep patterns we know are bad for them. It's loving to teach our children to get enough sleep and protect it for them until they believe it themselves.

Our American culture has a distorted belief about getting by on a few hours of sleep a night. Some believe it indicates a person is stronger or more resilient than the rest of us. It's as if we're competing and the one who gets the least sleep wins.

But the one who gets the least sleep loses.

◇ List a physical health challenge and describe how sleep affects it.

_____

_____

_____

_____

_____

◇ List a mental health challenge and describe how sleep affects it.

_____

_____

_____

_____

_____

◇ List a spiritual health challenge and describe how sleep affects it.

_____

_____

_____

_____

_____

_____

◇ What step will you take to assure you get adequate sleep tonight?

_____

_____

_____

_____

_____

Chapter Eleven

FREE YOUR MIND

CONNECT WITH OTHERS

We're social beings. This is a social universe. All things are connected to one another. We need deep and meaningful relationships to thrive in our lives.

There is a sense of relief when we're with others. We breathe a little easier. When we're with others, we get out of our own head and focus outside ourselves.

Being with others gives us a broader perspective. Every person has a unique set of circumstances that have shaped their lives. When we hear from others, our world expands.

◇ How do you engage with others on a weekly basis?

_____

_____

_____

_____

_____

◇ What does connecting with others do for you?

_____

_____

_____

_____

_____

◇ What does connecting with others do for them?

_____

_____

_____

_____

_____

CONNECT WITH SELF

In addition to connecting with others, we need to have a healthy connection with our self. What we think and say about ourselves is important for freeing our mind.

To be healthy and unstuck, it's crucial to know how to keep your thoughts positive.

◇ Are your thoughts about yourself primarily positive or negative? Describe them.

_____

_____

_____

◇ What do you think would be different in your life if you had more positive thoughts about yourself?

_____

_____

_____

If you lived with someone who constantly spewed negative comments about your dress, your coworkers, and your life, you'd want to stop living with them. The problem is, we can't stop living with ourselves. Our thoughts can subject ourselves to a kind of misery we would never want to inflict on anyone else.

Perfectionism is at the root of negative thinking. When we're striving for perfection, we become judgmental. Everyone is a rival or someone to compare yourself to. This leads to negative thinking.

◇ What can you do to improve your thought life?

_____

_____

_____

◇　How will you make a new and healthy thought process a habit?

_____

_____

_____

_____

WHERE THE TWO MEET

When you understand personal boundaries, you can navigate difficult relationships by understanding both what you're responsible for and what you're not responsible for.

There are rules in relationships, but we each have a slightly different version of them. The only rules we can enforce in relationships are the ones we have for ourselves. This is where personal boundaries come into play. When we take responsibility for ourselves, communicate clearly to others what we want, and stay consistent, all our relationships will be better.

Boundaries are best explained by using a physical example. Let's create an image in our minds to represent our lives, using physical aspects to represent different parts we're responsible for. Imagine your life as a yard. It stretches out in front of you. Everything in this yard is yours and yours alone.

EMOTIONS

The weather in your imaginary yard represents your emotions. We all have them. Just like the weather changes, sometimes our emotions seem to pop out of nowhere and derail our thoughts. Other times our emotions add extra pleasure to our activities. Either way, our emotions are ours to handle.

◇ How are you managing the weather (emotions) in your yard?

_____

_____

_____

_____

_____

◇ What are your emotions telling you about your thinking?

_____

_____

_____

_____

_____

◇ How will you manage your difficult emotions the next time they arise?

_____

_____

_____

_____

_____

There is a chair in your yard, which represents your attitude. It's the place you choose to sit.

Our attitude is our intention. It's what we decide when we wake up in the morning. It's what we say to ourselves before a big meeting. It's the anticipation we feel before dinner with friends.

Attitude is ours to control. When we don't control our attitude, we are likely to be like a chameleon and take on the attitudes of those around us. This indicates a boundary problem.

◇ What attitudes have you picked up from others which show a boundary problem?

_____

_____

_____

_____

_____

◇ Why do you pick up other people's attitudes instead of choosing your own?

_____

_____

_____

_____

◇ How will you choose your own attitudes instead of taking them on from others?

_____

_____

_____

_____

CHOICES

In your imaginary yard, you are holding a beverage. The beverage represents your choices. Think about how you spend your time and money, how hard you try at something new, and the investment you put into your friendships and family. We make these choices every day.

Many of us have put our minds on autopilot when it comes to our choices. We simply react to what's around us instead of choosing to pursue things that satisfy our deepest desires to be healthy and unstuck.

◇ What choices do you leave up to others? Why?

_____

_____

_____

_____

_____

◇ How can you begin to make your own choices?

_____

_____

_____

_____

_____

VALUES

As you sit in your chair, sipping on a beverage, you can look out into your yard and see something beautiful. This beautiful object represents your values.

It's important to identify what you value because it is something important for you to protect.

We get stuck when we have conflicting values with those around us and expect them to value what we do. Understanding happens when our conflicting values are seen simply as differences from one yard to the next. We allow each person to protect what they value without making them see things the same as we do.

When something is valuable to us, it's our responsibility to protect it. What you value is under your care. Protecting your values means saying no to anything that will compromise them.

◇ What do you value?

_____

_____

_____

_____

◇ What steps will you take to protect what you value?

_____

_____

_____

_____

GIFTS

Around your yard is a fence. Attached on the outside is something which represents your gifts. It is an expression of a healthy life sharing itself with the rest of humanity.

Strengthening, expanding, honing, and displaying our gifts is up to us. We are the only ones able to practice them over and over to get them right. We are the only ones who will have the passion and drive to bring them to fruition. And we are the only ones who can have the courage to share them with the world.

◇ What are your gifts?

_____

_____

_____

◇ How are you using your gifts?

_____

_____

_____

◇ How do you feel when using your gifts?

_____

_____

_____

_____

◇ How are your gifts serving others?

_____

_____

_____

MANAGING YOUR THOUGHTS

In the fence that surrounds your yard is a gate. It represents your ability to manage your thoughts. It has the ability to take what you hear from others and either keep those thoughts out or let them in. Like the stone-faced soldiers at Buckingham Palace, you decide which thoughts to let in and which to keep out.

At first this can be difficult work, but just like riding a bike, soon you are doing it automatically. The gate is your power. Don't leave it open, flopping in the wind.

Our thoughts are our responsibility. Other people may place thoughts in your mind, but once they arrive at your gate, they become yours to manage. Sometimes, like after the leaves have fallen in early autumn, we have cleanup to do. We need to get out the rake, put the leaves in bags, and bring them out to the curb.

◇ What negative thoughts do you need to take out to the curb?

_____

_____

_____

◇ Describe how you may have been boundaryless and allowed other people's thoughts to cause destruction in your yard.

_____

_____

_____

Many of us simply open the gate and leave it open, thinking this is the best way to share our lives. That's all fine and good, but if your yard gets destroyed as people tread all over it with no limits, no one will want to visit because it will have nothing to offer. If you allow others to mistreat you, steal what you value, negatively affect your attitude, hurt your feelings, alter your choices, and place unhealthy thoughts in your mind, you're not sharing your life but allowing it to be damaged and changed by those around you.

◇ Who is determining the position of your gate (the thoughts you accept)?

_____

_____

_____

_____

◇ How can you gain control of your gate (your thoughts)?

_____

_____

_____

_____

◇ How will you know if you've lost control of the gate (your thoughts) again?

_____

_____

_____

_____

The fence represents your boundary. Now that you know what resides in your yard, you'll be able to take responsibility for it. Your fence is the dividing line between your beautifully unique life and the lives of others.

◇ Picture your fence in your mind, then describe it below.

_____

_____

_____

_____

BOUNDARY PROBLEMS

Our behaviors are a place we exercise our boundaries, and they carry natural consequences. If we get enough sleep, we're sharp and ready to go the next day. If we manage our money, we have funds saved for an emergency. And if we invest in friendships, we both give and receive love.

What is important when talking about personal boundaries is recognizing what is ours and what is *not* ours. If a friend makes a poor choice and we step in to "take care" of the natural consequences, we do nothing but make sure they'll do it again.

We have a boundary problem.

This does not mean we don't support and continue to love. It just means we believe in them enough to succeed through their failures and show we are confident in their ability to bounce back.

◊ Which of your behaviors show you have a boundary problem?

_____

_____

_____

_____

_____

◊ Are people aware of your boundaries? Why or why not?

_____

_____

_____

_____

_____

◇ How can you communicate your boundaries clearly?

_____

_____

_____

◇ What limits would support your healthy boundaries? Why haven't you set those limits in the past?

_____

_____

_____

_____

◇ How can setting limits with others (healthy boundaries) help both you and those around you?

_____

_____

_____

_____

OWN YOUR LIFE

Blaming keeps you stuck. Unforgiveness keeps you in chains. When you realize your mental health depends on you, you own your life.

It takes courage to own the direction of your life. It is easier to say we didn't have the right opportunities, enough money, or enough time. But courage inspires us to look for and take opportunities.

Owning the direction of our life takes work and intention.

◇ What direction is your life going?

_____

_____

_____

_____

_____

◇ What can you do to take control of your life?

_____

_____

_____

_____

_____

◇ What work and intention will carry you to a new direction in your life?

_____

_____

_____

_____

_____

WORK ETHIC

Our work ethic is decided by how badly we want to get to where we're going. It's a measure of how much we're willing to pay and how much persistence we will have for what we want. In order to work toward something using a strong work ethic, we must first believe the work will accomplish something. Those with a strong work ethic don't expect others to do things for them.

A strong work ethic is foundational to pursuing *all* areas of health—physical, mental, and spiritual.

◇ How is your work ethic getting, or not getting, you what you want?

_____

_____

_____

_____

_____

◇ What abilities do you lack that you need to make up for with your work ethic?

_____

_____

_____

_____

_____

◇ What are some habits, skills, or routines that you have been unwilling to work at, but need to in order to get unstuck?

_____

_____

_____

_____

_____

DELAY GRATIFICATION

Another life skill to grow that will free your mind, allow you to live a healthy life, and get you unstuck is delaying gratification. Succumbing to our wants, wishes, and whims is often what got us stuck in the first place. Delaying gratification can be thought of as an investment. This turns what we may see as denying ourselves into a positive of what we will get out of it.

◇ What temptation are you gratifying?

_____

_____

_____

◇ What would you be investing in if you delayed this gratification?

_____

_____

_____

_____

◇ How can you delay gratification?

_____

_____

_____

_____

RESILIENCY

Being resilient when the storms of life hit is necessary to get and stay unstuck. Resiliency is not a trait people have or don't have. It involves behaviors, thoughts, and actions which can be learned and developed in anyone.

Research shows the primary factor in resilience is having caring and supportive relationships within and outside the family. Another way to increase our resilience is to not see our problems as insurmountable.

Resilience is also developed when we accept change as a part of life. Having this flexible attitude allows us to be nimble when obstacles present themselves.

◇ How resilient are you?

_____

_____

_____

_____

◇ What would make you more resilient?

_____

_____

_____

_____

◇ How is resilience connected to how you adjust to change?

_____

_____

_____

_____

BE PROACTIVE

Successful people don't wait for bad circumstances to show up before they take action to fix something that is almost broken. They buy toilet paper before they run out, have difficult conversations before emotions blow up, and practice gratitude when things are going well.

Our life is less stressful when we are proactive. When life inevitably throws a curveball at us, proactive people have a margin in their lives to handle it.

Being proactive also means not *reacting* to other people's aggressive, negative, or manipulative behavior. Proactivity defines our commitment to a sane mind. It listens and learns. It responds from a place of calm.

◊ What could you do to be proactive today?

_____

_____

_____

_____

_____

◊ How can you be proactive with your mental health?

_____

_____

_____

_____

_____

Chapter Twelve

FREE YOUR SPIRIT

FAITH

We all have faith. Many people have faith in a spiritual being. Others have faith in science. Some put their faith in an institution, and others have faith in themselves. Having faith means we know what we believe in and embrace it. We aren't tossed around by popular opinion. Our beliefs give us something to hold new ideas up to as a way to compare and assess. When we're confident in what we believe, we no longer have to defend our position but are peaceful in it.

◇ Who or what do you have faith in?

_____

_____

◇ Who or what don't you have faith in?

_____

_____

◊ How does your faith help you?

_____

_____

_____

_____

_____

◊ Describe the faith you have in yourself.

_____

_____

_____

_____

_____

GRATITUDE

Being grateful is an easy way to live. As we practice gratitude, the negative thoughts melt away, our heart becomes lighter, our mood becomes more desirable, and our smile shows up.

It takes effort and creativity to be grateful, but after the effort you will feel lighter and less burdened. In the long run, you will have a happier and more fruitful life.

Who would you rather be around: a person who complains about the weather, or a person who talks about how grateful they are to be alive? When we're grateful, more people will want to be around us.

It's impossible to be angry and grateful at the same time. The energy we feel when we're grateful is peaceful as opposed to the tense energy we feel when we're angry.

When gratitude becomes a habit, we will no longer need to exert so much energy to come up with an inventive way to see the positive. When we focus on the positives in a situation, we learn to act from a strong position. Instead of fear driving our decisions, we are in a capable, calm, and clear frame of mind.

◇ What are you grateful for today?

_____

_____

_____

_____

_____

_____

◇ How can listing what you're grateful for improve your mood?

_____

_____

_____

_____

_____

◇ How can you remind yourself to be grateful?

_____

_____

_____

_____

HOPE

Hope generates ideas, motivates people to act, and keeps us going when inevitable failures arrive. Hope is our rocket fuel. It propels us forward despite the obstacles we see or fear. Hope is necessary to climb over the challenges of life. Hope is a brand-new day with opportunities waiting to be discovered. Hope is a lifeline. Hope is your own. Hope is a choice.

Being hopeful frees our spirit. It's both a vulnerable and courageous place. Being hopeful is strong and attractive. It's playful yet serious. Hope is magical and the secret to success. It's a necessary characteristic to achieve big things. Hope is the antidote to fear. It isn't a strategy but a critical component for a great life.

◇ What will you hope for today?

_____

_____

_____

_____

◇ How can you develop your spiritual muscle of hope?

_____

_____

_____

_____

_____

_____

JOY

Joy is a combination of contentment and freedom. Wouldn't it be amazing to feel that all the time? You can.

Joy does not depend on your circumstances. Joy is a choice. It's always available and will be more readily accessible when we have a storage room full of it in our hearts.

Joy is an emotion we can choose.

◇ How do you describe the feeling of joy?

_____

_____

_____

_____

_____

_____

◇ Do you feel joy today? Why or why not?

_____

_____

_____

_____

◇ How can you feel joy on a daily basis?

_____

_____

_____

_____

MEANING

Meaning is the message we get from the events in our life. Seeing meaning in the circumstances of our everyday lives is a spiritual practice. It can make sense of the situation when things don't go well and provide understanding to events in our lives.

We can find meaning even in our failures. Without reflecting on what just happened, we're prone to make the same mistakes or stay in unhealthy life patterns.

Finding meaning can also free us from sorrow. The mistakes I've made over my life, although difficult, are freeing when I find meaning in them and understand the lessons they revealed.

Meaning is not always easy to find, but finding meaning in your circumstances will give you a fuller and richer life.

◇ What has been meaningful to you today?

_____

_____

_____

◇ What made it meaningful?

_____

_____

_____

◇ How will you find meaning in one difficult situation in your life?

_____

_____

_____

PURPOSE

Finding your purpose can be simple. Think about the things you do that feel good deep down in your spirit. They aren't necessarily easy or without trepidation, but you're in the zone when you're doing them. Time goes quickly. Motivation isn't a problem. You love to talk about them, read about them, and learn more about them.

Purpose is an internal push that is almost too powerful to resist. Your purpose is in your spirit and wants to show itself. It's more than an impulse. It's a drive. It's filled not with excitement but pursuit. It won't leave you alone until you acknowledge it.

Our lives are not simply a series of random events but a series of events that build on one another like a snowball rolling down a hill. This snowball gets bigger and stronger with each turn. It will reveal your purpose.

◇ List a series of events, good and bad, that brought you to where you are today. What are those events telling you about your purpose?

_____

_____

_____

_____

◇ Explain how you are using your past experiences to learn and take steps towards your purpose. What are you willing to give up to fulfill your purpose?

_____

_____

_____

_____

◇ How can your purpose give you freedom?

_____

_____

_____

_____

_____

LOVE

Loving ourselves and others is the solution to all our problems. It's the key to our happiness. Love is the basic element needed to be productive, help others, and live in peace.

We all need love. Even your curmudgeonly neighbor needs it. Your rebellious teenager needs it. The successful businessman needs it. You need it. The more we understand our need to both receive and give love, the healthier we will be.

If we're loving out of obligation or fear, it's like wearing a pair of skinny jeans that have no give. It hurts and we easily grow tired. We can hardly wait to take those stinkin' jeans off and put on yoga pants.

But when we love from the love we feel for ourselves, it's easy. We can only love others to the extent we love ourselves.

◇ How are you practicing the art of love?

_____

_____

_____

_____

◊ How can loving yourself improve the love you have for others?

_____

_____

_____

_____

◊ How can you take steps towards self-love?

_____

_____

_____

_____

We love both ourselves and others best when we are doing the thing we were created to do. This is where we operate best. When we're in this place, love flows from us. Our vocation is an extension of our love as we do whatever it is well, enjoy doing it, and serve others.

◊ How can your vocation show love?

_____

_____

_____

_____

_____

◇ Write up a job description for your ideal vocation.

_____

_____

_____

_____

_____

◇ What will you do to practice your vocation fully?

_____

_____

_____

_____

_____

Chapter Thirteen

SO NOW WHAT?

This is a lifelong journey for all of us. The beauty of this process is we can grow and become freer each day. We get to decide. The stuck places in our lives are not just bad karma but signposts pointing us toward greater health and freedom.

So now what? What have you acknowledged about why you are stuck? What steps have you determined will take you toward better health? How will you heal, strengthen, and free your body, mind, and spirit?

◊ How will you free your body?

_____

_____

_____

_____

_____

_____

◇ How will you free your mind?

◇ How will you free your spirit?

_____

_____

_____

_____

_____

_____

_____

This is good work. You have taken the time and put in the effort to answer the questions that reveal why you are stuck. No doubt you've discovered a lot about yourself along the way.

The investment you've made in yourself will pay off in your life. This process has taught you how to face what has you stuck so you can get unstuck. As you continue to ask yourself questions, you will be able to move forward no matter what circumstance comes your way. You never have to stay stuck again.

So Now What? is a lifestyle. It's an attitude. It's constantly asking what your next step should be. It's a belief that there is always another step. There is always another answer.

So Now What? is a journey. It's never done. There will always be something more to do, something more to learn, and something more to experience. It's a movement forward instead of being stuck.

So Now What? is a way of life. It starts with love of self. It's a method to heal, strengthen, and free your body, mind, and spirit. It will give you freedom.

ISBN 13: 978-1-63489-426-5

Library of Congress Catalog Number has been applied for.
Printed in the United States of America
First Printing: 2021

25 24 23 22 21   5 4 3 2 1

Cover design by Nupoor Gordon
Interior design by Shannon Nicole Plunkett

Wise Ink Creative Publishing
807 Broadway St NE
Suite 46
Minneapolis, MN, 55413

To order, visit www.itascabooks.com or call 1-800-901-3480.
Reseller discounts available.